THE
AMERICAN
REVOLUTION

MODERN CURRICULUM PRESS

◎ Program Consultants

SHARON HARLEY, PH.D.
Associate Professor/Acting Director
African American Studies
University of Maryland

STEPHEN MIDDLETON, PH.D.
Assistant Professor of History
North Carolina University

CHARLOTTE STOKES
Teacher Specialist, Social Studies
Alexandria, Virginia Public Schools

◎ Program Reviewers

JACOB H. CARRUTHERS, PH.D.
Professor/Associate Director
Center For Inner City Studies
Northeastern Illinois University

BARBARA EMELLE, PH.D.
Associate Director of
Curriculum and Instruction
New Orleans Public Schools

PAUL HILL, JR.
Executive Director,
East End Neighborhood House
Cleveland, Ohio

SUBIRA KIFANO
Teacher Advisor
Language Development Program
 for African American Studies
Los Angeles Public Schools

MARY SHEPHERD LESTER
Director of Mathematics
Dallas Public Schools

LINDA LUPTON
Curriculum Coordinator
Cleveland Public Schools

GWENDOLYN MORRIS
Instructional Support Teacher
Philadelphia Public Schools

THOMASINA PORTIS
Director, Multicultural/Values Education
Washington, D.C. Public Schools

DOROTHY W. RILEY
Librarian and Author
Detroit, Michigan

Illustrators
Lou Pappas, Chapter Bottom Borders; Mal Cann, 13, 29 (top); Dave Henderson, 30–31; Jennifer Hewitson, 42; Ron Himler, 24, 25, 34; Celina Hinojosa, 14–15, 22; Doug Knutson, 32–33, 39; Al Leiner, 20–21, 29; Rodica Prato, 38; Thom Ricks, 26–27, 28 (bottom); Gary Thomas, 35.

Photo Credits
4-5, 8, 9,11 (top), 22 (bottom left and bottom right), 35, 36 (top), 41, The Granger Collection; 6-7, 39, Library of Congress; 10, American Antiquarian Society; 11 (bottom), Bostonian Society; 14, 31, Massachusetts Historical Society; 17, Concord Museum; 18-19, The Bettmann Archive; 22 (top), Collection of Dr. Alexander A. McBurney, Kingston, RI; 23, Courtesy of The Old Print Shop, Inc.; 25, Leet Brothers; 34, Massachusetts State Archives; 36, (bottom) Raphaelle Peale/Absalom Jones, 1810, Delaware Art Museum, Wilmington, Gift of Absalom Jones School, 1965; 40, Pedro Coll/The Stock Market; 12 (top), By J.E. Taylor, 1897, New York Public Library, The Schomberg Collection; 12 (inset), U.S. Post Office.

Map Credits
4, 9, Ortelius Design; 16, 37, Ortelius Design and Rodica Prato.

Acknowledgments
Every reasonable effort has been made to locate the ownership of copyrighted materials and to make due acknowledgment.
Any errors or omissions will be gladly rectified in future editions.

Design & Production: TWINC, Catherine Wahl, Kurt Kaptur
Executive Editor: Marty Nordquist
Project Editor: June M. Howland

MODERN CURRICULUM PRESS
13900 Prospect Road, Cleveland, Ohio 44136
Simon & Schuster • A Paramount Communications Company

Based on *The African American Experience: A History* published by Globe Book Company © 1992.

ISBN 0-8136-4964-1(Paperback)   ISBN 0-8136-4963-3(Reinforced Binding)

10 9 8 7 6 5 4 3 2 1   98 97 96 95 94

CONTENTS

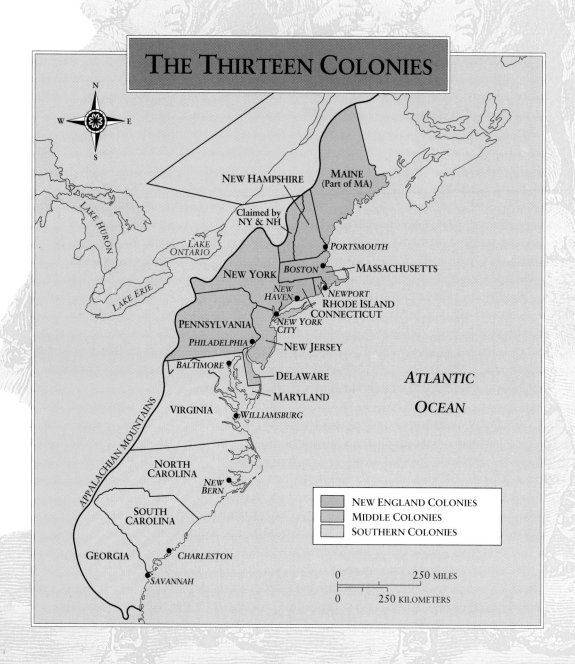

THE THIRTEEN COLONIES

NORTH

W   E

S

LAKE HURON

LAKE ONTARIO

LAKE ERIE

NEW HAMPSHIRE

MAINE (Part of MA)

Claimed by NY & NH

PORTSMOUTH

NEW YORK

Boston   MASSACHUSETTS

NEW HAVEN

NEWPORT

RHODE ISLAND

CONNECTICUT

NEW YORK CITY

PENNSYLVANIA

Philadelphia

NEW JERSEY

BALTIMORE

DELAWARE

MARYLAND

ATLANTIC

OCEAN

VIRGINIA

WILLIAMSBURG

APPALACHIAN MOUNTAINS

NORTH CAROLINA

NEW BERN

SOUTH CAROLINA

GEORGIA

CHARLESTON

SAVANNAH

	NEW ENGLAND COLONIES
	MIDDLE COLONIES
	SOUTHERN COLONIES

0   250 MILES

0   250 KILOMETERS

HISTORY
SPEAKS

In 1775, there were thirteen British *colonies*, or settlements, along the Atlantic coast of North America. African Americans made up about five hundred thousand of the total two and a half million people who lived in those colonies. There were also thousans of Native Americans. The African Americans, most of whom had been brought to America against their will, were very unhappy. Most were held in *bondage*. They did not have the personal independence that other *colonists* had.

For years many of the European people of the colonies had been content under British rule. Many had not. They welcomed the talk of independence they heard from other colonists. They wanted more of a say in governing their own land. Some people called *Patriots* even argued that the colonies should be free to rule themselves. African Americans wanted freedom as well—personal freedom.

When the war began, many African American colonists, both enslaved and free, sided with the Patriots. Others supported the British. Whichever side they chose, they were about to become part of an American Revolution—a fight for freedom. The roles African Americans played in that fight had a big effect on the outcome of the war.

1

A storm was brewing in America in 1775. African Americans had a keen interest in how the colonies and Great Britain would settle their differences. The ties between the colonies and Great Britain were strained and ready to break. The colonists had been arming themselves for months. All Americans waited and watched for the moment when they would be called upon to defend their protest against British controls.

Prince Whipple, one of many African Americans who supported the American Patriots, is shown rowing General Washington's boat. From the beginning, Africans were an important part of the colonists' struggle for freedom.

THE WAR BEGINS

It was early on the morning of April 19, 1775. Peter Salem, a young African American living in Massachusetts, suddenly sat up in bed and listened. There it was again. The clatter of horse's hooves, a voice shouting, "They're coming! The *Redcoats* are coming!" Peter quickly dressed. Other *Minutemen* of Framingham—men trained to defend their town "at a minute's notice"—were doing the same. What they had all feared, but were ready for, had happened. British soldiers, often called Redcoats, were marching toward the nearby town of Concord. The Minutemen lighted lanterns, reached for *muskets* and powder horns, and left their homes. They gathered in the center of town. Peter Salem, himself a freed African American, stood proudly among them. That day they would take part in the shooting that was the beginning of the American Revolution.

Peter Salem and others defend Concord from British attack.

The Battles of Lexington and Concord

Before noon, Peter Salem and the other Minutemen marched toward Concord eager to defend Patriot supplies stored there. Minutemen from other towns, young African Americans Cuff Whittemore, Job Potama, and Cato Bordman would join them. All of these men would face some seven hundred British soldiers.

The first gunshots of the *Revolution* had been heard earlier that morning. The British Redcoats had marched into Lexington, Massachusetts, firing on the seventy-seven Minutemen waiting there. When the gun smoke cleared, eight Americans had been killed and one British soldier had been hurt. The British then continued their march toward Concord. Here they would find some three hundred fifty Minutemen armed and ready.

As the British neared Concord's North Bridge, they opened fire on the Minutemen. Peter Salem and the others held their ground, firing back. The British began to retreat along the road to Boston. Patriots followed them, firing from behind fences and trees. African Americans Pomp Blackman, Isaiah Bayoman, and Cato Wood were among them. Prince Estabrook, who had faced the British earlier at Lexington, fell wounded. A group with David Lamson seized British supply wagons and took six British prisoners.

After sunset the British limped back into Boston. Their red coats were stained by sweat, dirt, and blood. Around two hundred fifty of them had been killed or wounded. The Minutemen had lost fewer than ninety men. It was, however, just the beginning.

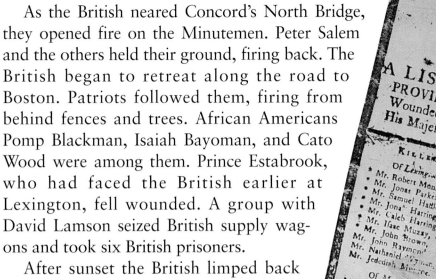

Look carefully to find Prince Estabrook's name on this list of injured soldiers.

LEXINGTON AND CONCORD

North Bridge

CONCORD

LEXINGTON

MEDFORD

LINCOLN

MENOTOMY

WESTON

WALTHAM

Bunker Hill

CHARLESTOWN

CAMBRIDGE

BOSTON

CHARLES R.

FRAMINGHAM

DORCHESTER HEIGHTS

BROOKLINE

CHARLES R.

ROXBURY

MYSTIC R.

CONCORD R.

- CITIES
— ROADS
— RIVERS
✸ BATTLES

0   5 MILES

0   5 KILOMETERS

The Battle of Bunker Hill

Two months later, the battle scene of Concord was repeated on a larger scale outside Boston. By June 16, 1775, the state *militias* from New Hampshire, Rhode Island, and Connecticut had gathered, trapping the British in the city. Even though these citizens, many of them African American, had little military training, they volunteered to fight. As yet there was no organized colonial army.

Led by Colonel William Prescott, African American Peter Salem was again part of these Patriot troops. About twelve hundred of them waited on Breed's Hill outside the city. At sunrise, June 17, 1775, at least twenty-two hundred British soldiers formed battle lines and began a steady march toward the Patriots.

In their *trenches* and behind fences and over on Bunker Hill, the Americans stood ready. The British moved closer and closer. Finally the order rang out from the American side. "Fire!"

Patriot guns blazed. What would become one of the bloodiest battles of the American Revolution had begun.

Colonists were called to volunteer for state militias. Why do you think there were more African volunteers from northern states than from southern ones?

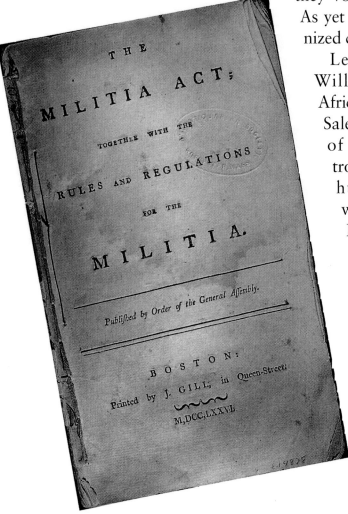

THE MILITIA ACT;

TOGETHER WITH THE

RULES AND REGULATIONS

FOR THE

MILITIA.

Published by Order of the General Assembly.

BOSTON:

Printed by J. GILL, in Queen-Street.

M,DCC,LXXVI.

The Battle of Bunker Hill. The European and African men on far right side of this painting were later put on a U.S. stamp.

THE BOSTON MASSACRE

The first African American to give his life for American freedom died years before the start of the war in 1775. He died at one particular event in 1770 that started colonists down the road to revolution.

On a cold winter evening, a small group of colonists stood on a Boston street shouting insults at a British soldier on patrol. The colonists took out all their anger at the British on these soldiers.

African American Crispus Attucks joined the group just as they started throwing snowballs at the soldier. British reinforcements appeared and from somewhere came the order to fire.

British guns were shot into the crowd. Suddenly five colonists lay dead, Crispus Attucks among them. This event added greatly to the colonists' hatred of the British.

Why do you think this event was called the Boston Massacre?

African Americans were in the thick of this fighting later known as the Battle of Bunker Hill. Several of them were praised for their courage. It was reported that Cuff Whittemore fought bravely to the end of the battle even after being wounded. Salem Poor is said to have fought well, too. Afterwards, the Patriot officers signed a letter praising Poor and calling him a "brave and gallant soldier."

Top: Peter Salem shoots Pitcairn during the Battle of Bunker Hill.
Inset: United States stamp honors Salem Poor.

Contributors To The Cause...

Salem Poor   *Gallant Soldier*

U.S. 10¢

Peter Salem won the greatest fame of any African American Patriot in the Battle of Bunker Hill. He and other Patriots stood face to face with the British as they made their last charge. British Major John Pitcairn shouted, "Surrender, you rebels. The day is ours!" Peter Salem took careful aim and fired. Pitcairn fell dead. The colonists continued the bloody battle but in the end were forced to retreat.

The Battle of Bunker Hill erased all hopes for peace between Great Britain and the colonies. The Patriots had sent a message to the rest of the world—they would fight to the death for the independence they so badly wanted.

A Continental Army

After the Battle of Bunker Hill, colonists realized they might be facing a long fight. An official *Continental army* was formed under the leadership of General George Washington.

Peter Salem and other African Americans who had fought with the militias became members of this army. That was not true of all African Americans. Each colony had its own opinion about whether or not to allow African Americans to enlist in the Continental army.

Owners of enslaved African Americans worried their slaves would be killed, costing them their valuable property. The owners also feared that armed slaves would rise up against them. Some even claimed that African Americans did not want to fight.

In most cases the opposite was true. Many Africans hoped that a victory for America's freedom would mean freedom from enslavement for them as well. Still the Continental army at first barred African Americans from enlisting.

Then in November, 1775, Lord Dunmore, a Loyalist of Great Britain and governor of Virginia, took a bold step. He promised freedom to any African Americans owned by Patriots who would fight for the British. Hundreds rushed to enlist. General Washington, commander of the Continental army, was worried to see the number of British troops grow. He suggested that the African Americans, who had already proven themselves in battle, be allowed to join his army. The colonial leaders finally agreed.

Flag given to honor the "Bucks of America" by John Hancock.

As the fighting dragged on into 1777, the Continental army welcomed any fit soldier—African or European, free or enslaved. A practice of sending substitute soldiers was also used. An American who did not want to fight in the Continental army could send another man, often an enslaved African, in his place. Many states eventually promised freedom to Africans who served in the army. The only states who did not enlist African American soldiers were Georgia and South Carolina.

Some colonial fighting units, such as the "Bucks of America," were all-African units. Rhode Island's First Regiment was one of the most well-known. This *regiment* led by Colonel Middleton, fought fiercely at the Battle of Rhode Island in 1778. It was reported that Germans who had joined the British troops refused to face them a second day. By the end of the war, over six thousand African Americans had fought in the Continental army.

African Americans serving as colonial soldiers, however, were not treated equally with the

European soldiers. All Africans entered the army as privates and few were ever promoted. They were usually given the oldest guns and clothing and were paid less than the European soldiers.

The well-trained British, with better equipment and supplies, won battles at Long Island, White Plains, and Ticonderoga. The Continental army, although not as experienced, won victories at Trenton, Princeton, and Saratoga. Lack of money and supplies would be a problem for colonists throughout the Revolution.

African Americans did more than fight for the colonies. They dug trenches, built forts, drove supply wagons, and built roads. Some of them served as guides, blacksmiths, *wheelwrights*, and carpenters. These support jobs played a key role in helping the Americans continue their fighting. African American women also aided the Continental army. They cooked food for the soldiers and helped care for the wounded, often on the battlefields.

What's Your Name?

African Americans rarely were allowed to use their African names when they came to the colonies. Enslaved Africans were given new names by their owners at the time of their purchase.

The first names commonly given were short and came from the *Bible*, history, or other literature. The most popular male slave names were: Jack, Tom, Harry, Sam, Will, and Caesar.

The most common women's names were: Bet, Mary, Jane, Hanna, Bett, and Sarah. If a last name was ever needed, enslaved people used the last names of their owners.

Those African Americans who were free often took names of those whom they admired or of past owners. The most common last names during this time were: Williams, Jones, Johnson, Smith, Jackson, and Thomas. Later, freed African Americans, such as Elizabeth Freeman, took names that said something about their beliefs and hopes for freedom.

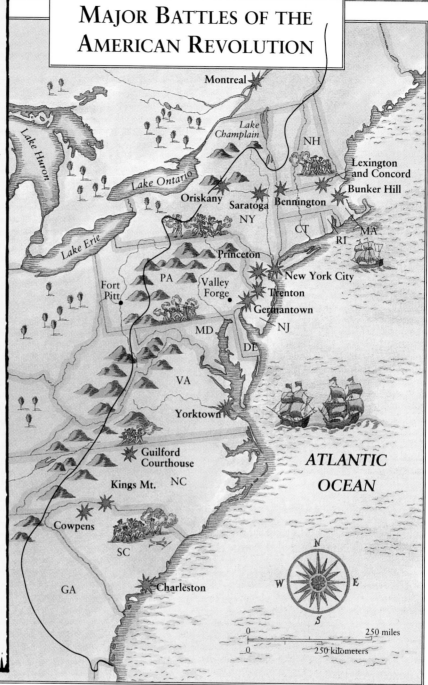

Major Battles of the American Revolution

Throughout the revolutionary war, what African Americans cared most about was very plain. Personal freedom and liberty were the things for which they were fighting. The African American names freed men were able to choose for themselves made this point: Cuff Liberty, Pomp Liberty, Dick Freedom, Peter Freeman, Jube Freeman, and Jupiter Free.

TALK ABOUT IT

◎ After the Battle of Bunker Hill, how do you think the European Minutemen felt about the African Americans in their units?

◎ Why were the support jobs filled by African Americans so important to the first battles of the Revolution? Which of these jobs do you think were the most important or most helpful to the colonists? Why?

◎ Why do you think the British were at first more eager to have African Americans join their army than the colonists were? If you had been a colonial general, how would you have handled the question of whether or not African Americans could enlist in your army?

WRITE ABOUT IT

You are a radio announcer on the scene of the Battle of Concord or Bunker Hill. You are the eyes and ears of the listening audience. Write your news report as you would give it as an eyewitness to the action of one of these battles.

2

As the war between the colonies and Great Britain continued, African Americans were hoping that whatever the outcome, they would be given their liberty. They looked to the colonial government, hoping that the laws created in a free nation would bring them freedom. During the summer of 1776, **delegates** from the thirteen colonies drafted an official **Declaration of Independence**. It was a major step in the colonial struggle for freedom. However, it did not help African Americans gain freedom.

These two privateer ships were part of the colonial fighting forces on the sea. Because the Continental navy was small, these private ships helped protect America from British ships during the Revolution.

The Struggle Continues

On July 8, 1776, a large crowd gathered outside the Pennsylvania State House in Philadelphia. The African Americans in the group listened as the commander of the militia read from the *Declaration of Independence*. On the outer edges of the crowd stood a ten-year-old African American boy named James Forten. He listened as these words rang out: "All men are created equal," and all people have rights to "life, liberty, and the pursuit of happiness." As the commander finished reading, the crowd burst into cheers. Cannons boomed. Church bells rang out and continued all night. James Forten, an African American who had been born free, cheered the loudest of all. Just four years later, Forten himself would join the fight for colonial liberty.

What Forten and others would realize, however, is that they had cheered too soon. The *Declaration of Independence* had completely overlooked the problem of freeing Africans held in bondage.

The War at Sea

Many brave Patriots fought the British on the sea as well as on land. African Americans were welcomed in the newly-formed Continental navy and served on the ships: *Providence*, *Alliance*, *Alfred*, *Boston*, and *Ranger*. The navy was more in need of workers to support their fighting men than the army was.

The navy was assisted by state navies and by *privateers*, privately owned boats. In 1780, at the age of fourteen, James Forten joined the crew of a privateer, the *Royal Louis*. The duty of privateers was to capture British merchant ships and their cargoes. Almost thirteen hundred privateers roamed the seas during the war.

Being young and quick, James served as a powder boy aboard the *Royal Louis*. He was one of twenty

African Americans in the crew of two hundred. For James, the job paid more than the four dollars a month he had earned as a shop clerk. Also, crews of privateers shared in the profits from captured British cargoes. James needed money to support his mother and sister since his father had died.

At first the *Royal Louis* was successful in battle. Then the privateer's luck changed. Sailing the eastern coast of America, it came upon three British warships. Even though outnumbered, the Royal Louis faced them and prepared to fight. Canon balls flew. Guns fired. The crew of the *Royal Louis* fought bravely but was outnumbered and had to surrender.

A CHAMPION FOR EQUAL RIGHTS

Prince Hall, an African American, was a man of his word—and his words were often on petitions and protests to the American government. During the war years and after, he was a champion fighting for the rights of all African Americans.

• Hall was one of the first to argue that the United States, fighting for its own freedom, should not hold African people in bondage. His protests caused the Continental army to change its early policy of not enlisting African Americans.

• When European Americans refused him membership in a group that stood for the brotherhood of all men, the Freemasons, he started his own African American freemason group.

• Being self-educated and realizing the importance of education, he petitioned the government to organize schools for African American children. Because of Hall's efforts, African American children first attended free schools in 1797.

James Forten was taken aboard the British ship *Amphyon* as a prisoner. His fear was that he would be sold into slavery. However, the captain of the *Amphyon* felt sympathy for James since he too had a son who happened to be on board. The two boys became friends. The son asked his father to let James come back to England with them. The captain agreed, but

An African American who served in the Continental navy.

James refused. "No! No!" he replied. "I am here a prisoner for the liberties of my country. I never, never shall prove a traitor to her interests."

James was sent to one of the prison ships anchored off the coast of New York. Captured Patriot sailors were crammed onto these floating prisons for months at a time. Thousands did not survive. James Forten did, living for eight months aboard the *Jersey*, one of the worst ships. After the war ended, he returned to Philadelphia and took up his father's trade of sailmaking. He earned a small fortune and spent much of it to bring an end to slavery in the United States.

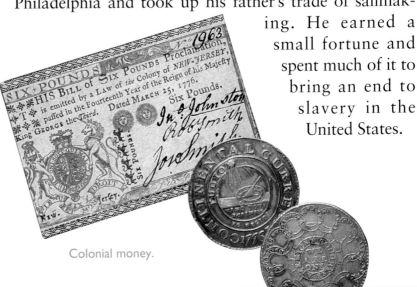

Colonial money.

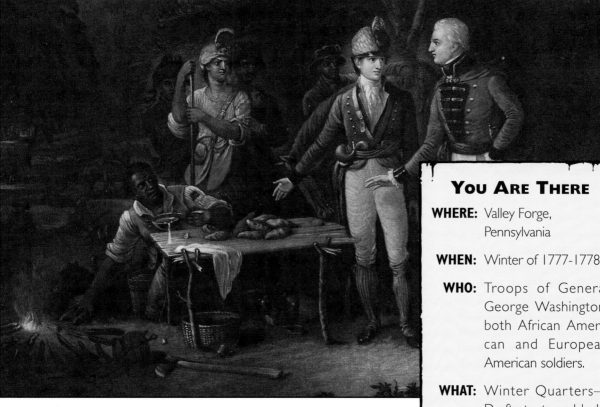

American general "Swamp Fox" Marion had an African aide. What do you think the aide might overhear?

Behind Enemy Lines

Throughout the war, African Americans battled shoulder to shoulder with European colonists. Some of the bravest of those who fought for the Patriot cause never fired a gun. Still they met the enemy face to face. They were the Patriot spies.

Often working for British soldiers, African Americans could move around their camps without being noticed. They were trusted and could see and hear things no one else could. The Patriots used this to their own advantage, asking some African Americans to secretly report information about British troops. These spies risked their lives passing information to the Continental army. Anyone caught spying by the British was hanged.

You Are There

WHERE: Valley Forge, Pennsylvania

WHEN: Winter of 1777-1778

WHO: Troops of General George Washington, both African American and European American soldiers.

WHAT: Winter Quarters—Drafty tents and leaky shelters protect you against the snow and wind. Food supplies are constantly low. You are served a Thanksgiving dinner of rice and vinegar. You, and many others, do not have coats, shoes, or blankets. Your feet are wrapped in rags, often leaving bloody tracks in the snow. A great number of soldiers around you are dying from *typhus,* starvation, and the cold. Meanwhile the British forces stay in comfortable quarters in nearby Philadelphia.

The most famous African American spy was James Armistead of Virginia. In 1781, Armistead volunteered to be a spy for the Patriots. However, this task became much more complicated and dangerous than he ever imagined. Armistead worked for the Marquis de Lafayette, a French supporter of the colonists. Lafayette worked closely with General George Washington. After Washington's terrible winter at Valley Forge in 1778, more foreign countries had come to the aid of colonists.

After a time, Lafayette sent Armistead away claiming he no longer needed him. The African American then found a job working for Lord Cornwallis, the British commander. Cornwallis quickly learned to value Armistead's quick mind and asked him to spy for the British. Armistead agreed. What Cornwallis did not know, nor did anyone but Lafayette, was that James was still working for the Patriots—as a spy. Now he had become a double spy!

Members of General Washington's staff, African and European, were present when he met the defeated British.

With the help of Armistead and the French troops, Washington was able to defeat Cornwallis' forces at Yorktown in 1781. This would be the last major battle of the revolutionary war. The final treaty between Great Britain and America was not signed until 1783. At the end of the war, the government of Virginia made James Armistead a free man. He then took the name James Armistead Lafayette in honor of his former commander.

Supporting the British

Many African Americans turned to the British with their hopes of freedom. As a minister wrote, many enslaved Africans "secretly wished that the British army might win, for then all *Negro* slaves will gain their freedom."

It is not known exactly how many African Americans sided with the British. Some historians say over five hundred of them had joined British troops following Lord Dunmore's offer of freedom in 1775. Thousands more Africans fled *plantation* life, seeking freedom behind British troop lines.

As the war continued, some volunteered for all-African American fighting units set up by the British. African Americans also served on British ships and acted as guides. Native Americans also served in this way. Their knowledge of the country's land and seacoast was very valuable. Other Africans worked on and off the battlefield as wagon drivers, blacksmiths, cooks, and carpenters.

In 1781, a British general said, "These Negroes have undoubtedly been of greatest service." In all, thousands of African men and women aided the British. Whatever their roles, their goal was the same as that of Africans who supported the colonists. They all hoped for an end to enslavement.

By 1782, British troops began to leave the United States. The truce agreement between the two countries stated that the British could not take any American property with them when they left.

WHERE IS ESCHIKAGON?

In the summer of 1780, one "handsome Negro," was reported taken prisoner by a British officer looking for information on French troops in the area around Lake Michigan. Jean Baptist Point du Sable, an African from Haiti, had years earlier set up a trading post on the north bank of the Chicago River.

He was the first African in the area and one of the first to trade with Native Americans there. Soon realizing there was money to be made in trading for furs with the native tribes, du Sable built a successful business.

Known for his fair business dealings, du Sable was well-respected by Europeans and Native Americans alike. The spot du Sable chose to build his trading post was called Eschikagon (eh SHEEK uh gahn) by the Native Americans. It grew, prospered and eventually became one of the great cities of the midwest United States. Which city do you think du Sable settled?

Still, many African Americans who had been loyal to the British were aboard British ships when they sailed. As one British officer said, "We cannot in justice abandon [them] to the merciless [anger] of their former masters."

These African Americans sailed off to new lives in Great Britain, Canada, Jamaica, and the Bahama Islands. Some went as far away as Germany as part of the German forces that had fought with the British. Many African Americans were forced to leave with their owners who had supported the British. Altogether, nearly twenty thousand African Americans left the United States after the war. ◈

TALK ABOUT IT

◎ Why do you think James Forten joined the battle for independence at such a young age? How was his life similar to or different than the lives of fourteen-year-olds today?

◎ After he had been captured, James Forten refused the British captain's offer of a safe home in England. Why? What would you have done if you had been in his place?

◎ What do you think was the most important way African Americans aided the Patriots during the revolutionary war?

WRITE ABOUT IT

James Forten spent months on a prison ship. Imagine you are James writing a letter to his mother, as he might have. Tell her where you are, how you got there, and how you feel as a prisoner of war.

3

African Americans joined in every major battle of the American Revolution, showing bravery and loyalty to their fellow soldiers. The Battle of Yorktown in 1781, marked the end of the actual fighting of the war. A peace agreement between Great Britain and the United States was not signed until 1783. Some battles fought by African Americans during these war years were not fought on a battlefield. In 1781, in a small Massachusetts town, an enslaved African American woman fought for her freedom in a court of law.

Many Americans showed their anger over unfair British and American laws by speaking out against them. Free speech was one right every American valued.

A MATTER OF JUSTICE

The words of Mum Bett, an African American woman held in bondage, tell how much she longed to be free.

"Anytime, while I was a slave, if one minute's freedom had been offered to me, and I had been told I must die at the end of that minute, I would have taken it just to stand one minute on God's earth a free woman—I would."

Mum Bett and her younger sister, Lizzie, were children when they were bought in 1758, by Colonel John Ashley, a rich merchant.

These sisters worked in the Ashley home in Sheffield, Massachusetts, until a summer day in 1781. Then their lives suddenly changed. Mrs. Ashley had become angry at Lizzie, attacking her with a hot fireplace shovel. Mum Bett stepped quickly between them and was burned on the arm. She fled the Ashley home, leaving Lizzie behind and swearing she would never return. Immediately, Mum Bett saw this as the opportunity for which she had been waiting. It was time to claim her freedom under the law.

Mum Bett had been thinking about this plan ever since she had heard the promises of the new constitution of the state of Massachusetts. Although she could not read or write, she had paid close attention to conversations in the Ashley home about Massachusetts law. She hoped the law would help her if she could get her case heard by the court. Mum Bett first had to find a lawyer willing to help. Knowing that he was taking on a difficult battle,

Theodore Sedgwick agreed to represent her. A workman named Brom, also owned by Ashleys, joined Mum Bett in her bid for freedom.

In court, Sedgwick pointed out that according to the Massachusetts constitution, "all men are born free and equal." He argued that this meant slavery was not legal in Massachusetts. In an unexpected decision, the jury agreed with Sedgwick. Mum Bett and Brom were free, and Colonel Ashley was ordered to pay a fine. After 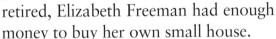 winning the case, Mum Bett changed her name to Elizabeth Freeman. For many years after that, she had a paid job caring for the Sedgwick family. When she retired, Elizabeth Freeman had enough money to buy her own small house.

CULTURE CORNER

THE FIRST AFRICAN AMERICAN BAPTIST CHURCH

African American churches have always supported freedom. When and where did these churches start?

In the mid-1700s, an enslaved African American named David George escaped. Eventually he was caught and sold onto a plantation in Georgia. There he learned to read using the *Bible*.

In around 1775, George and other African Americans formed the first African American Baptist church at Silver Bluff, Georgia. There, George preached his message of the hope for freedom for all people.

After the war was over, George moved to Canada, where he started a new Baptist church. Then, in 1792, he sailed to West Africa and founded the first Baptist church there. Why do you think the churches have supported fighting for freedom?

The Move to End Slavery

Following the end of the war, thousands of African Americans like Elizabeth Freeman turned to the state courts for freedom. Others sent *petitions*, or written requests, to state governments who had not passed antifreedom laws. Some African Americans received freedom for serving in the Continental army.

Thousands simply ran away from their owners. Some were allowed to enter Canada. Some joined American Indian groups, such as the Seminole Indians of Florida or others in the West.

Many African Americans were returned to slavery after the war. Thousands of workers were needed to keep the huge southern plantations going. Because southern slave owners strongly controlled the state governments, slavery remained firmly in place.

Africans signed petitions and sent them to state governments to gain freedom.

An early pamphlet written to convince Americans to stop slavery. What famous American printed this pamphlet?

However, the seeds of freedom had been planted. Americans who believed slavery was wrong began to form antislavery groups long before the war had ended. These groups of both Africans and Europeans worked for the *abolition*, or ending, of slavery.

Philadelphia became the first center of *antislavery* action. Pennsylvania had a larger population of African Americans than any other northern state. The "Pennsylvania Society for Promoting the Abolition of Slavery and the Relief of Free Negroes" had been started there in 1775. It was the first antislavery group in the world and had many Patriots among its members.

SOME
CONSIDERATIONS
On the KEEPING of
NEGROES.
Recommended to the PROFESSORS
of CHRISTIANITY of every
DENOMINATION.

By JOHN WOOLMAN.

PHILADELPHIA:
Printed and Sold by JAMES CHATTIN,
in Church-Alley. 1754.

Richard Allen

After the war ended, the society sent antislavery petitions to the government. They refused to buy products made by enslaved African Americans. They even paid some slave owners to free their workers held in bondage. The society also helped African Americans who had been freed. They started education classes for children and adults and helped those who were jobless to find work.

Laws to end slavery began in the northern states. In 1777, Vermont had become the first northern state to pass such a law. Within the next few years, all northern states passed some antislavery laws.

Even in the North, however, life was not easy for African Americans. Some cities would not allow African children to attend public schools. Many employers would not hire African workers. Even churches were not fair to Africans. They often made them sit in separate areas during services.

In 1787, an antislavery group made up of African Americans was started by ministers Richard Allen and Absalom Jones. Their "Free African Society" of Philadelphia was the first organized group of African Americans. Both of these men had been born into slavery and had later earned their freedom.

Absalom Jones

Their ideas to help one another and their community spread. Soon groups like it became active in New York City, Boston, and Newport, Rhode Island.

In Philadelphia, in 1787, delegates from twelve of the new states met to draw up a constitution for their nation. Americans waited to see if this new document would include the antislavery laws some of them thought were needed. They were to be disappointed.

The *Constitution of the United States*, which went into effect in 1789, promised "the blessings of liberty" to the people of the nation. However, those blessings were not given to free or enslaved African Americans.

	Free African Americans			Free African Americans	
	1790	1990		1790	1990
Massachusetts	5,369	223,681	Virginia	12,866	1,011,025
Rhode Island	3,484	27,754	Maryland	8,043	969,181
Connecticut	2,771	219,375	North Carolina	5,041	1,443,672
New Hampshire	630	4,292	Delaware	3,899	96,034
Maine	536	3,428	South Carolina	1,801	939,412
Vermont	269	1,283	Georgia	398	1,806,107
Pennsylvania	6,531	1,060,333	Tennessee	361	7,336,261
New York	4,682	2,710,674	Kentucky	114	270,822
New Jersey	2,762	933,699			

The Constitution did not abolish slavery or end the Atlantic slave trade, and it required states to return runaway slaves. In fact, the word "slave" did not appear in the Constitution. Delegates instead used the phrase "persons held to service or labor."

By 1790, there were more than seven hundred fifty thousand African Americans in the United States. Eight of every ten of these African Americans were in bondage, most of those living in the southern states. The U.S. census made the first official count of free African Americans in 1790. The chart (left) shows where these free African Americans lived.

The establishment of the Constitution showed that Americans who believed in abolition still had a long fight ahead of them. Many years would pass and more blood would be shed before liberty for all Americans would be a reality. Jupiter Hammon, an enslaved preacher and poet, wrote:

"That liberty is a great thing we . . . know from our own feelings . . . I must say that I have hoped that God would open their eyes, when they were so much engaged for liberty, to think of the state of the poor blacks . . ."

PAUL
CAPTAIN
CUFFEE
1812.

WE WON'T PAY!

"It's not fair—we aren't allowed to vote but we're expected to pay taxes!" the angry crowd grumbled among themselves. Statements such as these were heard from Africans as the United States began setting up its own laws.

In 1780, Paul Cuffe took a stand. Within days of going to jail himself for not paying his taxes, he appealed directly to the Massachusetts legislature. He argued that since African Americans had "no voice in the election of those who tax us" they should not be forced to pay the taxes.

Born in Massachusetts in 1759, Paul Cuffe, was one of the first voices for African American rights heard by colonial lawmakers.

The Massachusetts legislature eventually added a statement to its constitution giving African Americans the same rights as the other people of Massachusetts. This included the right to vote.

A HOME IN FREETOWN

Some African Americans returned to their homeland after the Revolution. Thomas Peters was an African American who had sided with the British during the Revolution. He and others had been promised freedom and land by Great Britain. After the American victory, Peters and other African Americans went to Nova Scotia, Canada. There the British gave them freedom, but no land.

For years afterward, Peters demanded the British fulfill their promises. By the time British officials agreed, in the late 1780s, Peters had a new idea. He had heard that a freedom settlement for African Americans had been started in Africa. Peters convinced other African Americans to join him in going there.

In March, 1792, fifteen ships from Canada landed at Sierra Leone, on Africa's west coast. Aboard were Peters and eleven hundred other African Americans seeking new lives. They joined in the building of a settlement called Freetown. Today Freetown is the capital of Sierra Leone.

This is a busy market in Freetown, Sierra Leone today. The settlement made by African Americans has grown and prospered. How do you think the first settlers felt about coming to live here?

The difficult problem of dealing with the issue of slavery continued. Leaders were worried that this issue might divide the country. Lawmakers in the North gave in to demands from Southerners that slavery be allowed to continue in the United States.

The Constitution also limited one hope for freedom that many enslaved people had—escape. The document stated that even though a slave might escape to a free area—one that did not have legal slavery— they remained slaves. Their owners could claim them any-where in the country.

So the American Revolution came to an end on a dis-appointing note for African Americans. Those who had fought the hardest would benefit the least by the American victory. For the next two hundred years, African Americans would continue their struggle for their own independence and freedom. 🪕

Some ideas were added to the Constitution after it was written. What do you think African Americans at this time would have added?

TALK ABOUT IT

◎ Mum Bett knew it would be difficult to get fair treatment in court because she was enslaved. What other things about Mum Bett and her case do you think might have hurt her chances of getting fair treatment? How do you think courts today are different than courts in the 1780s?

◎ After the war, how do you think African Americans who sided with the colonists felt about the African Americans who sided with the British?

◎ Do you think the Revolution made life better or worse for African Americans in the United States? Why?

WRITE ABOUT IT

You were the court reporter on the day Elizabeth Freeman's case was decided. You took careful notes of everything that was said. Write the statement the jury might have made as they announced their final decision in this matter.

ECHOES

OF EARLY AFRICA

The stories of African Americans in the revolutionary war involve many brave heroines and heroes. These people found themselves in situations of drama and danger. What experiences of theirs were most interesting to you? Which of these colonial African Americans would you like to read more about?

At the time of the Revolution, not every African American agreed with the ideas of the Patriots. If you had been an African American colonist at that time, with whom would you have sided—the Patriots or the British? Why?

At the end of this war, African Americans were left with an ongoing struggle for freedom. What difference has this made in the lives of African Americans today? What would you have added to the Constitution to address the needs of African Americans?

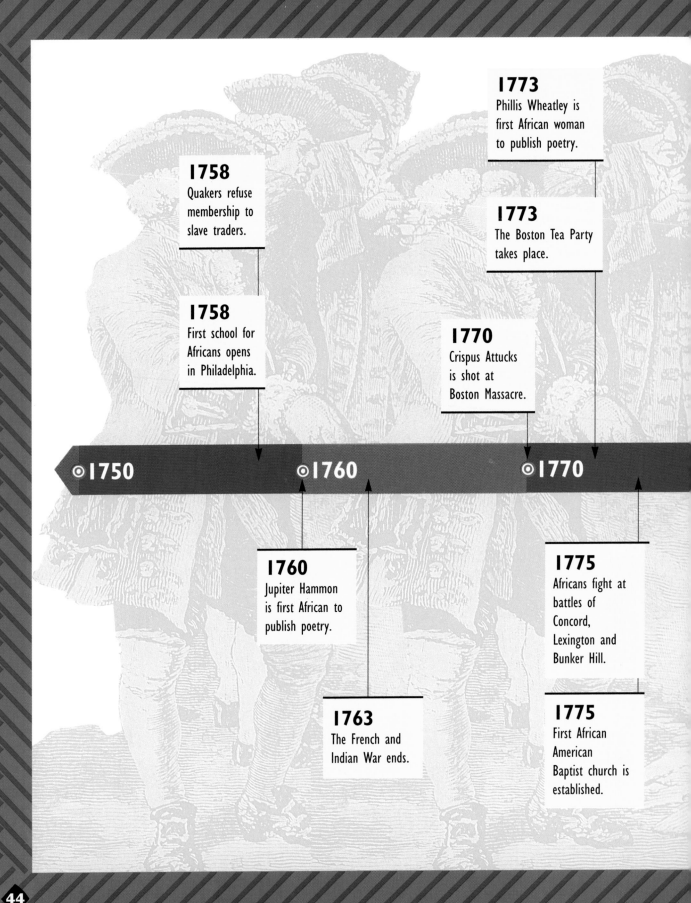

1773
Phillis Wheatley is first African woman to publish poetry.

1758
Quakers refuse membership to slave traders.

1773
The Boston Tea Party takes place.

1758
First school for Africans opens in Philadelphia.

1770
Crispus Attucks is shot at Boston Massacre.

⊚**1750**   ⊚**1760**   ⊚**1770**

1760
Jupiter Hammon is first African to publish poetry.

1775
Africans fight at battles of Concord, Lexington and Bunker Hill.

1763
The French and Indian War ends.

1775
First African American Baptist church is established.

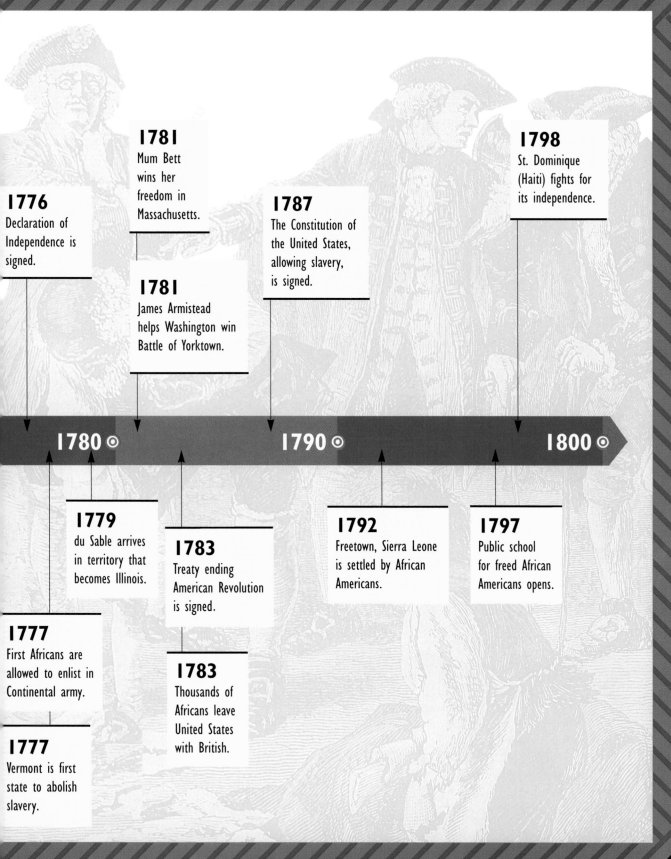

1776
Declaration of Independence is signed.

1781
Mum Bett wins her freedom in Massachusetts.

1781
James Armistead helps Washington win Battle of Yorktown.

1787
The Constitution of the United States, allowing slavery, is signed.

1798
St. Dominique (Haiti) fights for its independence.

1780 ◎   **1790** ◎   **1800** ◎

1779
du Sable arrives in territory that becomes Illinois.

1783
Treaty ending American Revolution is signed.

1792
Freetown, Sierra Leone is settled by African Americans.

1797
Public school for freed African Americans opens.

1777
First Africans are allowed to enlist in Continental army.

1783
Thousands of Africans leave United States with British.

1777
Vermont is first state to abolish slavery.

GLOSSARY

abolition • (ab uh LIHSH un) • The movement to end slavery in the United States before the Civil War.

antislavery • (an teye SLAY vur ee) • Against the practice of holding people in bondage.

bondage • (BAHN dij) • Being held or controlled completely by another person.

colonist • (KAHL uh nist) • A person who settles in a new area.

colony • (KAHL uh nee) • A place that is settled and governed by a country that is a distance away.

Continental army • (kahn ti NEN tul AR mee) • The first national army organized by the colonists during the American Revolution.

Declaration of Independence • (dek luh RAY shun uv ihn dee PEN duns) • Document written by the American colonists that stated the reasons why they wanted their independence from Great Britain.

delegate • (DEL uh gayt) • A representative.

enslavement • (in SLAYV munt) • The practice of holding another person in bondage.

Loyalist • (LOI uhl ist) • A colonist who supported Great Britain during the American Revolution.

militia • (muh LIHSH uh) • A volunteer group of soldiers made up of citizens.

Minutemen • (MIHN iht men) • A group of American citizens trained to fight at "a minute's notice."

musket • (MUHS ket) • A gun with a long barrel, used by soldiers and others before the rifle was invented.

Negro • (NEE groh) • A term first used by Europeans to describe Africans; from Spanish word for black.